JOHN CLARE

THE POET AND THE PLACE

". . . For everything I felt a love,
The weeds below, the birds above;
And weeds that bloomed in summer's hours
I thought they should be reckoned flowers
They made a garden free for all,
And so I loved the great and small . . ."

JOHN CLARE *The Progress of Rhyme*

JOHN CLARE

THE POET AND THE PLACE

PETER MOYSE

THE CROSSBERRY PRESS, HELPSTON

TO MARY

©1993 THE CROSBERRY PRESS
The Stables, 1a West Street
Helpston, Peterborough, PE6 7DU

Photographs ©1993 Peter Moyse, ARPS

Typeset in Monotype Baskerville
and printed in England by
WITLEY PRESS LTD
Hunstanton, Norfolk, PE36 6AD

ISBN 0 9520714 0 1

FOREWORD

Few writers have given such an intensely detailed and personally visualised account of their native territory as John Clare, and to complement his words with photographs might at first seem a daring act. But these are no ordinary photographs for the one all-important reason that they are the work of a man so steeped in the poet's landscape that his pictures have become one of the best aids for seeing it as Clare must have seen it. Because Clare confined his vision to his own parish, what he saw became the most authentic view which we possess of rural England at large as it existed before mechanised farming. His poetry is an elegy for this England, even as Improvement and the railways began its destruction. Unlike so many mourners of a changing scene, Clare had an expert understanding of the countryside. Everything from its ecology to its working practices, its cultural traditions to its archaeology fed his 'song'. No other writer has left us with every step, as it were, of his movements in the home fields. Thus, there is scarcely a yard of Helpston and its environs which does not say something to the Clare reader and create in him a kind of reverie. The fact that half his life was spent in exile from Helpston only deepened Clare's sense of belonging to this one place, and nowhere else, which is a common feeling, although hard to put into words. John Clare's work celebrates what he believed should have been common to all countrymen and women, an intelligent look at everything which lay around them.

In spite of the years and in spite of countless changes, many of the places which Clare loved are still recognisable to the reader, as indeed are the places which caused him suffering. There are two maps, one of paradise by inheritance, the other of paradise lost. Peter Moyse's photographs provide a wonderfully sensitive guide to what remains of a countryside which formed England's greatest rural poet. Peter Moyse and his wife Mary live in Helpston where, over the years they can be said to have walked with Clare in a way which has given them a tender and authoritative knowledge of his path, she with her tracing of the poet's family roots, he with a camera. The pictures are a reminder of Clare's walking pace, also his use of the local landscape as an inexhaustable inspiration for his art. They capture its modesty and provoke in us, today's Clare-seekers, an intent to look more carefully at what might otherwise have escaped our eye. Thomas Hardy was still living when a neighbour began to photograph his Wessex. John Clare would no doubt have been amazed that, a century and a half after his death, an ever-growing readership for what he had to say itself finds inspiration in his native lanes and fields, but it is so. These beautiful photographs lead us on.

Ronald Blythe 5

ACKNOWLEDGEMENTS

First of all, I wish to thank Garbriel Woolf, President of the Alliance of Literary Societies, for encouraging me to publish this book by subscription, and the subscribers who have made the venture possible. My thanks too, to Ronald Blythe for writing the foreward and Professor Eric Robinson and Professor Kelsey Thornton for their support and advice. I also want to thank Trevor Lockwood, of Author-Publisher Enterprise, who has given freely of his technical knowledge and expertise; Alan and Chris Witley of Witley Press, Hunstanton who have been most understanding printers for a novice publisher to work with; fellow members of the John Clare Society, who have been enthusiastic about the production of this book in John Clare's Bicentenary Year and my wife Mary, for her skill and patience in getting the manuscript ready for publication.

Peter Moyse
Helpston, December 1992

Note: John Clare's spelling and punctuation (or lack of it) in the extracts printed in this book are, as far as possible, in the form used by John Clare himself. The extracts have been chosen from published editions of his work transcribed from the original manuscripts.

INTRODUCTION

John Clare (1793-1864), a contemporary of Shelley (1792-1822) and Keats (1795-1821) was not an ordinary man, and certainly not an ordinary poet. He was an acute observer of nature. His real concerns were the ravages of over-intensive cultivation and the shrinking access to the countryside he was intimately associated with, and loved so well. These concerns arouse similar emotions today, indeed, his writing so full of powerful visualisation, is readily accessible to the modern reader. In his day, Clare witnessed drastic changes in the landscape, his landscape, with the impostion of the Enclosure Acts in the early 1800's.

"... Inclosure like a Buonparte let not a thing remain
It levelled every bush & tree & levelled every hill
& hung the moles for traitors – though the brook is running still
It runs a nake(d) brook cold & chill ..."

Today, many of Clare's favourite haunts have long disappeared. With the spread of urbanisation, changes of agricultural use, the recent ravages of Dutch Elm disease, whole acres of woodlands, places where he used to hear the song of the nightingale, and where he used to find the first primrose of spring, are no more. A number of old hedgerows have disappeared, under *"The ravages of the blundering plough"*. New roads have been built. A change of land use has ultimately altered its character. Tall steel towers carrying essential power cables now straddle the horizons. The railway, the main rail artery from London, and soon, from the Continent, speeding with an incessant 'swish' of the high speed snake-like Inter City trains to the North, bisects the countryside. Above, the sudden roar of low flying jet warplanes startles the visitor.

In spite of all this, there are some surprises left, one, mercifully preserved, and managed by The Countryside Commission, is the area beloved by Clare as 'Emmonsales Heath', but now known as the Castor Hanglands, where, under their sympathetic custodianship, the landscape is left unchanged. In 1990, the Peterborough City Council arranged for a number of roadside verges to be protected from indiscriminate cutting and in this way has enabled a number of the traditional wild flowers to return to the hedgerows and overspill into the fields and verges as well. This measure, combined with the restrictions in the use of poisonous chemicals on the land, has resulted in the revival of an abundance and variety of the traditional wild flowers that form the East Anglian landscape.

About twelve years ago I became interested in the relationship between the literary and the visual landscapes, especially those in which a 'sense of place' has coloured the imagination of some of our major British authors. For example, Margaret Drabble and Jorge Lewinski's book,

'A Writer's Britain', Kim Taplin's 'The English Path'. David Daiches and John Flower's 'Literary Landscapes', the evocative 'Divine Landscapes' by Ronald Blythe, and Flora Thompson's 'Lark Rise to Candleford'.

In this small book, I have tried to portray this 'sense of place' in relation to the life and work of the poet, John Clare, with a selection of my monochrome photographs. The project started as a small folio of a few photographs related to, and illustrating some of Clare's poems, put together for the John Clare Society's first Annual John Clare Festival in Helpston in 1982. In this way the Society has given me much encouragement. Gradually, I developed a compelling desire to find out more about this remarkable man. I read the biographies of John Clare, namely, 'John Clare, a Life', by Anne Tibble, the earlier biography by Frederick Martin, published in 1865, a year after Clare's death, and 'Green Shadows' by June Wilson. In 1892, a new and excellent biography of Clare was written by Edward Storey, called 'A Right to Song', in which contains much recently discovered information and more importantly, dispels a number of myths.

The exploration of the countyryside around Helpston, aided by the excellent Ordnance Survey maps, helped me to retrace, as far as it was possible, some of Clare's favourite walks. Crossberry Way is still there, with its narrow path winding its way over stiles westward to the Roman road, King Street, and on to the hamlet of Ashton. The Torpel Way, a long distance footpath, linking Peterborough to Stamford, passes through a large part of Clare's countryside and follows a number of Clare's favourite walks. John Clare's Cottage still stands in Woodgate, Helpston. Now an attractive family home, it is not obvious that in Clare's day it was divided into five dwellings, two of them only accessible from the rear. Only two public houses are now left in the village of Helpston; The Blue Bell and The Exeter Arms, making attractive settings for the visiting Morris dancers at the John Clare Festival each July.

The predominant feature of Clare's countryside is its flatness. With such a vast expanse of sky, one is conscious, especially on sunny days, of following the sun's journey from horizon to horizon, there being no hills or large buildings to block its path. At first glimpse the landscape appears featureless, no great landmarks to give it scale. Only the tall spires of distant churches on the horizon attact our attention, the elegant tapering spire of St. Benedict's Church at Glinton being an example, often referred to by Clare. He went to school there for a time and the classroom was in the Lady Chapel of that church.

In many of Clare's poems he gives us a view of an intimate landscape, a landscape in 'microcosm' as I have heard it described. He noticed the simple beauty of the country, the small flowers, the common daisy, the shepherd's purse, 'a weedling wild', a field of beans, the scents after a fall of rain. 'the cloud bedappled sky' and the reflections from sunlight on water; his poetry is full of these joys.

I have enjoyed retracing some of John Clare's journeys into the countryside; the writings began to take on a new meaning. There were times when a sort of 'magic' would occur and the very poetry would spring into life, and almost jump out of the book. It was as if he had been watching me. Clare was very fond of pictures and the artist Peter De Wint was a friend of his.

He admired a painting by De Wint, and asked for a small picture of his to put up in his cottage. I have often wondered what he would have made of the camera and photography. There is a photograph of Clare, taken when he was in the asylum in Northampton, but I have not yet traced any comment by him about it.

Photography remains a magical and fascinating part of my life. It has given me an appreciation of light, form, pattern and motion, gifts that remain with me even when I do not have a camera with me, and that is not very often. The photography of Clare's landscape and the continuing inspiration of his poetry is a never ending theme. There is still a lot of work for me to do. It was however John Clare's wish that in the future, people would read his poetry, enjoy it, and associate it with the special landscape that made it possible. The following extract from 'Memory' in 'The Midsummer Cushion' by John Clare, edited by Anne Tribble and Kelsey Thornton, expresses Clare's feelings.

MEMORY

I would not that my being all should die
& pass away with every common lot
I would not that my humble dust should lie
In quite a strange & unfrequented spot
By all unheeded & by all forgot
With nothing save the heedless winds to sigh
& nothing but the dewy morn to weep
About my grave far hid from the worlds eye
I feign would have some friend to wander nigh
& find a path to where my ashes sleep
Not the cold heart that merely passes bye
To read who lieth there but such that keep
Past memories warm with deeds of other years
& pay to friendship some few friendly tears

It was this theme in mind I was compelled to retrace the footsteps of John Clare and produce these pictures.

In 1877 Thomas Hardy wrote in his notebook, 'The ultimate aim of the poet should be to touch our hearts, by showing us his own.' John Clare has certainly fulfilled that wish, and, in my own small way, with this book, I hope that he will never be *"by all unheeded & by all forgot"*.

Peter Moyse
Helpston 1992 9

John Clare in 1828, Behnes Bust, Northampton Central Library

I AM

I am - yet what I am, none cares or knows;
    My friends forsake me like a memory lost:–
I am the self-consumer of my woes;–
    They rise and vanish in oblivion's host,
Like shadows in love's frenzied stifled throes:–
And yet I am, and live – like vapours tost

Into the nothingness of scorn and noise,–
    Into the living sea of waking dreams,
Where there is neither sense of life or joys,
    But the vast shipwreck of my lifes esteems;
Even the dearest, that I love the best
Are strange – nay, rather stranger than the rest

I long for scenes, where man hath never trod
    A place where woman never smiled or wept
There to abide with my Creator, God;
    And sleep as I in childhood, sweetly slept,
Untroubling, and untroubled where I lie,
The grass below – above the vaulted sky.

Crossberry Way

From REMEMBRANCES

. . . When jumping time away on old crossberry way
    & eating awes like sugar plumbs ere they had lost the may
    & skipping like a leveret before the peep of day . . .

The Path to Eastwell Spring

From SUMMER IMAGES

. . . I love to walk the fields they are to me
    A legacy no evil can destroy
    They like a spell set every rapture free
    That cheered me when a boy
    Play pastime all times blotting pen consceals
    Come like a new born joy
    To greet me in the fields . . .

Reeds and Grasses

From *[SUMMER]*

How sweet when weary dropping on a bank
Turning a look around on things that be
Een feather headed grasses spindling rank
A trembling to the breeze one loves to see . . .

Bramble Spear

From THE BRAMBLE

Spontaneous flourisher in thickets lone
Curving a most impenetrable way
To all save nutters when a tree has shown
Ripe clusters to the autumns mellow day
& long the brustle of the rude affray
Clings to thy branches – scraps of garments torn
Of many hues red purple green & grey
From scrambling maid who tugs the branches down
& inly smiles at the strange garb she wears . . .

Footpath in Summer

STRAY WALKS

How pleasant are the fields to roam & think
Whole sabbaths through unnoticed & alone
Beside the little molehill skirted brink
Of the small brook that skips oer many a stone
Of green woodside where many a squatting oak
Far oer grass screeds their white stained branches hing
Forming in pleasant close a happy seat
To nestle in while small birds chirp & sing
& the loud blackbird will its mate provoke
More louder yet its chorus to repeat
How pleasant is it thus to think & roam
The many paths scarce knowing which to chuse
And full of pleasant scenes – then wander home
& oer beautys we have met to muse

The Path to Etton

FIELD THOUGHTS

Field thoughts to me are happiness & joy
Where I can lye upon the pleasant grass
Or track some little path & so employ
My mind in trifles pausing as I pass
The little wild flower clumps by nothing nurst
But dews & sunshine & impartial rain
& welcomly to quench my summer thirst
I bend me by the flaggy dyke to gain
Dewberrys so delicious to the taste
& then I wind the flag fringed meadow lake
& mark the pike plunge with unusual haste
Through water weeds & many a circle make
While bursts of hapiness from heaven fall
There all have hopes here fields are free for all

Through the Castor Hanglands

From EMMONSALES HEATH

. . . O who can pass such lovely spots
    Without a wish to stray
    & leave lifes care a while forgot
    To muse an hour away

    Ive often met with places rude
    Nor failed their sweet to share
    But passed an hour with solitude
    & left my blessing there . . .

In the Castor Hanglands

From EMMONSALES HEATH

In thy wild garb of other times
I find thee lingering still
Furze oer each lazy summit climbs
At natures easy will

Grasses that never knew a scythe
Waves all the summer long
& wild weed blossoms waken blythe
That ploughshares never wrong

Stern industry with stubborn pride
& wants unsatisfied
Still leaves untouched thy maiden soil
In its unsullied pride . . .

. . . Ive stretched my boyish walks to thee
When maydays paths were dry
When leaves had nearly hid each tree
& grass greened ancle high . . .

A Loiterer on the Barley's Beard

From INSECTS

Thou tiney loiterer on the barleys beard
& happy unit of a numerous herd
Of playfellows the laughing summer brings
Mocking the sunshine in their glittering wings
How merrily they creep & run & flye
No kin they bear to labours drudgery
Smoothing the velvet of the pink hedge rose
& where they flye for dinner no one knows . . .

Grass Plats

WOOD PICTURES IN WINTER

The woodland swamps with mosses varified
& bullrush forrests bowing by the side
Of shagroot sallows that snug shelter make
For the coy more hen in her bushy lake
Into whose tide a little runnel weaves
Such charms for silence through the choaking leaves
& whimpling melodies that but intrude
As lullabys to ancient solitude
– The wood-grass plats which last year left behind
Weaving their feathery lightness to the wind
Look now as picturesque amid the scene
As when the summer glossed their stems in green
While tasty hare brunts through the creepy gap
Seeks their soft beds & squats in safetys lap

Molehill, Castor Hanglands

From THE FLITTING

. . . I love the muse who sits her down
    Upon the molehills little lap
    Who feels no fear to stain her gown
    & pauses by the hedgerow gap
    Not with that affectation praise
    Of song to sing & never see
    A field flower grow in all her days
    Or een a forests aged tree . . .

34

A Clump of Fern

From THE CLUMP OF FERN

Pleasures lie scattered all about our ways
Harvest for thought & joy to look & glean
Much of the beautiful to win our praise
Lie where we never heeded aught had been
By this wood stile half buried in the shade
Of rude disorder – bramble woodbine all
So thickly wove that nutters scarcely made
An entrance through – & now the acorns fall . . .

Autumn

A AUTUMN MORNING

The autumn morning waked by many a gun
Throws oer the fields her many coloured light
Wood wildly touched close tanned & sutbbles dun
A motley paradise to earths delight
Clouds ripple as the darkness breaks to light
& clover fields are hid with silver mist
One shower of cobwebs oer the surface spread
& threads of silk in strange disorder twist
Round every leaf & blossoms bottly head
Hares in the drowning herbage scarcely steal
But on the battered pathway squats abed
& by the cart rut nips her morning meal
Look where we may the scene is strange & new
& every object wears a changing hue

Totter-grass on a Stone Wall

INSECTS

The insect world amid the suns and dew
Awake and hum their tiny songs anew,
And climb the totter-grass and blossom's stem
As huge in size as mighty oaks to them;
And rushy burnets on the pature rise
As tall as castles to their little eyes;
Each leaf's a town and the smooth meadow grass
A mighty world whose bounds they never pass;
E'en spots no bigger than a husbandman's
Or shepherd's noontide dwarf-shrunk shadow spans
–Or e'en the milkmaid tripping through the dew,
Each space she covers with her slender shoe–
Seems to their view high woods in which they roam
As lorn, lost wanderers many miles from home,
Creeping up bents and down whole weary hours
And resting oft on the soft breasts of flowers;
Till age, in minutes long as years, creeps on,
Or waning summer warns them to be gone.

Castle Clouds

FRAGMENT
(From a specimen of Clare's rough drafts)

The settled clouds in ridges lie
And some swell mountains calm and high
Clouds rack and drive before the wind
In shapes and forms of every kind
Like waves that rise without the roars
And rocks that guard untrodden shores
Now castles pass majestic bye
And ships in peaceful havens lie
These gone ten thousand shapes ensue
For ever beautiful and new

Rainclouds near Etton

SONG

The rain is come in misty showers
The landscape lies in shrouds
Patches of sunshine like to flowers
Fall down between the clouds
And gild the earth else where so cold
With shreds like flowers of purest gold

And now it sweeps along the hills
Just like a falling cloud
The cornfields into silence stills
Where musty moisture shrouds
And now a darker cloud sweeps o'er
The rain drops faster than before . . .

St. Benedict's, Glinton from the Fields

GLINTON SPIRE

Glinton thy taper spire predominates
Over the level landscape – & the mind
Musing – the pleasing picture contemplates
Like elegance of beauty much refined
By taste – that almost deifys & elevates
Ones admiration making common things
Around it glow with beautys not their own
Thus all around the earth superior springs
Those straggling trees though lonely seem not lone
But in thy presence wear superior power
& een each mossed & mellancholly stone
Gleaning cold memories round oblivions bower
Seem types of fair eternity – & hire
A lease from fame by thy enchanting spire

Stormclouds near Helpston

From Written in a Thunderstorm July 15th 1841

. . . This twilight seems a veil of gause and mist
    Trees seem dark hills between the earth and sky
    Winds sob awake and then a gusty hist
    Fanns through the wheat like serpents gliding bye
    I love to stretch my length 'tween earth and sky
    And see the inky foliage oer me wave
    Though shades are still my prison where I lie
    Long use grows nature which I easy brave
    And think how sweet cares rest within the grave . . .

The Approaching Storm

From Written in a Thunderstorm July 15th 1841

The heavens are wrath – the thunders rattling peal
Rolls like a vast volcano in the sky
Yet nothing starts the apathy I feel
Nor chills with fear eternal destiny

My soul is apathy – a ruin vast
Time cannot clear the ruined mass away
My life is hell – the hopeless die is cast
And manhoods prime is premature decay

Roll on ye wrath of thunders – peal on peal
Till worlds are ruins and myself alone
Melt heart and soul cased in obdurate steel
Till I can feel that nature is my throne . . .

Winter Landscape near Helpston

From WINTER IN THE FENS

So moping flat and low our valleys lie
So dull and muggy is our winter sky
Drizzling from day to day dull threats of rain
And when that falls still threating on again
From one wet week so great an ocean flows
That every village to an island grows
And every road for even weeks to come
Is stopt and none but horseman go from home . . .

Sunset over the Castor Hanglands

SUNSET

Welcome sweet eve thy gently sloping sky
& softly whispering wind that breaths of rest
& clouds unlike what daylight galloped bye
Now stopt as weary huddling in the west
Each by the farewell of days closing eye
Left with the smiles of heaven on its breast
Meek nurse of weariness how sweet to meet
Thy soothing tenderness to none denied
To hear thy whispering voice – ah heavenly sweet
Musing & listening by thy gentle side
Lost to lifes cares thy coloured skies to view
Picturing of pleasant worlds unknown to care
& when our bark the rough seas flounders through
Warming in hopes its end shall harbour there

Sunset at Helpston

[HOW BEAUTIFUL IS SUNSET EYE & BREAST]

How beautiful is Sunset eye & breast
Is filled with extacys & love & joy
The georgius liverie the glorious west
Is one short glance of heaven from the Sky

Wood Anemones and Celandines

WOOD ANEMONES AND CELANDINES

From *The Journal, 25th March 1825*

I took a walk to day to botanize and found
that the spring had taken up her dwelling
in good earnest she has covered the woods
with the white anemonie which the children
call Lady smocks and the hare bells are just
venturing to unfold their blue dropping bells
the green is covered with daiseys and the
little Celandine . . .

Wood Anemone in Royce Wood

WOOD ANEMONIE

The wood anemonie through dead oak leaves
And in the thickest woods now blooms anew
And where the green briar, and the bramble weaves
Thick clumps o'green anemonies thicker grew
And weeping flowers, in thousands pearled in dew
People the woods and brakes, hid hollows there
White, yellow and purple hued the wide wood through
What pretty, drooping weeping flowers they are
The clip't frilled leaves the slender stalk they bear
On which the drooping flower hangs weeping dew
How beautiful through april time and may
The woods look, filled with wild anemonie
And every little spinney now looks gay
With flowers mid brush wood and the hugh oak tree

Pale Primrose, Castor Hanglands

From THE PRIMROSE

Welcome, pale primrose starting up between
Dead matted leaves of ash and oak, that strew
The every lawn the wood the spinney through
Mid creeping moss and ivy's darker green
How much thy presence beautifies the ground
How sweet thy modest unaffected pride
Glows on the sunny bank and the woodland side

Cowslip, Castor Hanglands

From APRIL

. . . The shepherds on thy pasture walks
The first fair cowslip finds
Whose tufted flowers on slender stalks
Keep nodding to the winds
And tho thy thorns withold the may
Their shades the violets bring
Which childern stoop for in their play
As tokens of the spring . . .

Cow Parsley and Threatening Clouds

From WILD FLOWERS

Beautiful mortals of the glowing earth
And children of the season crowd together
In showers and sunny weather
Ye beautiful spring hours
Sunshine and all together
   I love wild flowers

The rain drops lodge on the swallows wing
Then fall on the meadow flowers
Cowslips and enemonies all come with spring
Beaded with first showers
The skylarks in the cowslips sing
   I love wild flowers . . .

Corn Poppy

From THE SHEPHERD'S CALENDAR – MAY

. . . Each morning now the weeders meet
To cut the thistle from the wheat
And ruin in the sunny hours
Full many wild weeds of their flowers
Corn poppies that in crimson dwell
Called 'head achs' from their sickly smell . . .

The Common Spotted Orchid

THE COMMON (SPOTTED) ORCHID

From *The Journal, Saturday 4th June 1825*

"Saw three fellows at the end of Royce wood who I found were laying out the plan for an 'Iron rail way' from Manchester to London – it is to cross over Round Oak Spring by Royce Wood Corner for Woodcroft Castle I little thought that fresh intrusions woud interupt & spoil my solitudes after the Inclosure they will despoil a boggy place that is famous for Orchises at Royce Wood end"

Dog Rose

DOG ROSE

From *Northampton MSS*

The wild hedge rose, its a bonny flower
As ever met the sunshine and the sky,
Its gold threads beaded with the summer showers
That patter on the glossy leaves and lie
Like pearls . . .

Spear Thistle

SPEAR THISTLE

Where the broad sheepwalk opens bare and brown
    With scant grass ever pining after showers,
And unchecked winds go fanning up and down
    The little strawy bents and nodding flowers,
There the huge thistle, spurred with many thorns,
The sun crackt upland's russet swells adorns.

Not undevoid of beauty there they come,
    Armed warriors, waiting neither suns nor showers,
Guarding the little clover plots to bloom
    While sheep nor oxen dare not crop their flowers
Unsheathing their own knobs of tawny flowers
When summer commeth in her hottest hours.

The pewit, swopping up and down
    And screaming round the passer-by,
Or running o'er the herbage brown
    With copple crown uplifted high
Loves in its clumps to make a home
Where danger seldom cares to come . . .

Butterfly on Wild Marjoram

WILD MARJORAM

From *The Journal, Thursday 21st October 1824*

". . . clumps of wild Marjoram are yet in flower about the mole hilly banks & clumps of meadow sweet linger with a few bunches yet unfaded"

Harebells on a Sunny Bank

HAREBELL

From *The Journal, Thursday 21st October 1824*

". . . took a walk in the fields – gathered a bunch of wild flowers that lingered in sheltered places as loath to dye – the ragwort still shines in its yellow clusters – & the little heath bell or harvest bell quakes to the wind under the quick banks & warm furze . . ."

Rooks Nesting

[ROOK'S NEST]

The rooks begin to build and pleasant looks
The homestead elms now almost black with rooks
The birds at first for mastership will try
They fight for sticks and squabble as they flye
And if a stranger comes they soon invade
And pull his nest in pieces soon as made
The carrion crow and hawk dare never come
They dare to fight like armys round their home
And boughs will hardly bear their noisy guests
And storms will come and over turn the nests
They build above the reach of clauming clowns
They climb and fast but cunning cuts them down
Others with reaching poles the nest destroys
While off and up they flye with deafening noise

Toad, Castor Hanglands

[I LOVE THE LITTLE POND TO MARK AT SPRING]

I love the little pond to mark at spring
When frogs and toads are croaking round its brink
When blackbirds yellow bills gin first to sing
And green woodpecker rotten trees to clink
I love to see the cattle muse and drink
And water crinkle to the rude march wind
While two ash dotterels flourish on its brink
Bearing key bunches children run to find
And water buttercups they're forced to leave behind

Sunlit Leaves on Water

From SONG

Swamps of wild rush beds and sloughs squashy traces
Grounds of rough fallows wi thistle and weed
Flats and low vallies of king cups and daiseys
Sweetest of subjects are ye for my reed
Ye commons left free in the rude rags of nature
Ye brown heaths be cloathed in furze as ye be
My wild eye in rapture adores e'ery feature
Yere as dear as this heart in my bosom to me . . .

Reed Patterns

THE SLEEP OF SPRING

I love the weeds along the fen
More sweet than garden flowers
For freedom haunts the humble glen
That blest my happiest hours
Here prisons injure health and me
I love sweet freedom and the free

An Old Willow Near Woodcroft

From THE OLD WILLOW

. . . How pleasant neath this willow by the brook
    Thats kept its ancient place for many a year
    To sit & oer these crowded fields to look
    & the soft dropping of the shower to hear
    Ourselves so sheltered een a pleasant book
    Might lie uninjured from the fragrant rain
    For not a drop gets through the bowering leaves
    But dry as housed in my old hut again
    I sit & troubleous care of half its claim decieve

The Lake, Lolham

THE MEADOW LAKE

                . . . Ive looked
In rapture on the mellow summer shine
Of the still water gleaming in the sun,
Just wrinkled by the plash of quiet kine
Who knee deep in the flags would drink – and done
Back to their feed on the shorn sward again;
The flags, the bulrush, and the barbed leaf
Of water weed, bethread with lighter vein . . .

Woodland Path, Lolham

From THE WOODS

I love to roam the woods
Oft patted by the boughs
That meet from either side
& form an arch of leaves
Till hidden as it where from all the world
I stand & muse upon the pleasant scene

I seem to be myself
The only one that treads
The earth at such a time
So vacant is the mass
That spreads around me one hugh sea of leaves
& intertwining grains of thickest shades . . .

Fallen Branch, Castor Hanglands

NOTHINGNESS OF LIFE

I never pass a venerable tree
Pining away to nothingness & dust
Ruins vain shades of power I never see
Once dedicated to times cheating trust
But warm reflection makes the saddest thought
& views lifes vanity in cheerless light
& sees earths bubbles youth so eager sought
Burst into emptiness of lost delight
& all the pictures of lifes early day
Like evenings striding shadows haste away
Yet theres a glimmering of pleasure springs
From such reflections of earths vanity
That pines & sickens oer lifes mortal things
& leaves a relish for eternity

A Recently Severed Tree Stump

From LANGLEY BUSH

. . . I looked upon its naked stump,
    And pictured back the fallen tree
    To days I played hop, skip and jump
    As happy as a boy could be.
    I turned me to that happy day
    I streaked beneath its mossy bough,
    And there came shadows of dismay,
    So dismally, I feel it now . . .

Ivy Round an Old Tree Trunk

TO THE IVY

Dark creeping Ivy, with thy berries brown,
    That fondly twist in ruins all thine own
Old spire-points studding with a leafy crown
    Which every minute threatens to dethrone;
With fearful eye I view thy height sublime,
    And of with quicker step retreat from thence
And thou, in weak defiance, strivst with Time,
    And holds't his weapons in a dread suspence.
But, bloom of ruins, thou are dear to me,
    When, far from danger's way, thy gloomy pride
Wreathes picturesque around some ancient tree
    That bows his branches by some fountain side:
Then sweet it is from summer suns to be
With thy green darkness overshadowing me.

A 'Pulpit' Tree, Helpston

THE HOLLOW TREE

How oft a summer shower hath started me
To seek for shelter in an hollow tree
Old hugh ash dotterel wasted to a shell
Whose vigorous head still grew & flourished well
Where ten might sit upon the battered floor
& still look round discovering room for more
& he who chose a hermit life to share
Might have a door & make a cabin there
They seemed so like a house that our desires
Would call them so & make our gipsey fires
& eat fields dinners of the juicey peas
Till we were wet and drabbled to the knees
But in our old tree house rain as it might
Not one drop fell although it rained till night

John Clare's Cottage, Helpston

From NOVEMBER

The village sleeps in mist from morn to noon
And if the sun wades thro tis wi a face
Beamless and pale and round as if the moon
When done the journey of its nightly race
Had found him sleeping and supplyed his place
For days the shepherds in the fields may be
Nor mark a patch of sky – blindfold they trace
The plains that seem wi out a bush or tree
Whistling aloud by guess to flocks they cannot see . . .

A Winter Blanket

WINTER

The small wind wispers thro the leafless hedge
Most sharp and chill while the light snowey flakes
Rests on each twig and spike of witherd sedge
Resembling scatterd feathers – vainly breaks
The pale split sunbeam thro the frowning cloud
On winters frowns below – from day to day
Unmelted still he spreads his hoary shroud
In dithering pride on the pale travellers way
Who croodling hastens from the storm behind
Fast gathering deep and black – again to find
His cottage fire and corners sheltering bounds
Where haply such uncomfortable days
Makes musical the woodsaps frizzling sounds
And hoarse loud bellows puffing up the blaze

104

After the Storm

From SNOW STORM

Winter is come in earnest and the snow
In dazzling splendour – crumping underfoot
Spreads a white world all calm and where we go
By hedge or wood trees shine from top to root
In feathered foliage flashing light and shade
Of strangest contrast – fancys pliant eye
Delighted sees a vast romance displayed
And fairy halls descended from the sky
The smallest twig its snowy burthen wears
And woods oer head the dullest eyes engage
To shape strange things – where arch and pillar bears
A roof of grains fantastic arched and high
And little shed beside the spinney wears
The grotesque zemblance of an hermitage . . .

Evening Light, St. Botolph's Churchyard, Helpston

From THOUGHTS IN A CHURCHYARD

Ah happy spot how still it seems
Where crowds of buried memorys sleep
How quiet nature oer them dreams
Tis but our troubled thoughts that weep
Lifes book shuts here its page is lost
With them & all its busy claims
The poor are from its memory crost
The rich have nothing but their names

There rest the weary from their toil
There lye the troubled free from care
Who through the strife of lifes turmoil
Sought rest & only found it there
With none to fear his scornful brow
There sleep the master & the slave
& heedless of all titles now
Repose the honoured & the brave . . .

John Clare's Gravestone, St. Botolph's, Helpston

MEMORY

I would not that my being all should die
& pass away with every common lot
I would not that my humble dust should lie
In quite a strange & unfrequented spot
By all unheeded & by all forgot
With nothing but the heedless winds to sigh
And nothing but the dewy morn to weep
About my grave far hid from the worlds eye
I feign would have some friend to wander nigh
& find a path to where my ashes sleep
Not the cold heart that merely passes bye
To read who lieth there but such that keep
Past memories warm with deeds of other years
& pay to friendship some few friendly tears

SUBSCRIBERS

Revd. D. A. Abraham

Mr & Mrs J. M. Anderson

Barbara Andrew

Patricia F. Arnett-Harris

Laurie Arnold

Mr R. E. Arnold

Revd Raymond Ashling

E. Winifred Avison

Jennifer Bancroft

Mary Bannister

Tom Bates

Angela & Alan Beeken

Joseph & Elizabeth Belmonte

Sheila F. Birch

Rev. Brian Blade

John Blagden

Irene Bleach

Mrs C. M. Blunden

William J. & Pamela F. Bomford

Roger H. Breeze

May Bright

Mrs M. Brooks

Peter Brown

Jean Bryson

Christina Bunce

Joan Burgess

Richard Burleigh

Mrs Ella Kathleen Burton

Ann Campbell

Mrs M. Carlile

Mr J. L. Carr

Evelyn A. Carroll

Mr R. C. Carter

Mrs D. M. Chaplin

Dr. T. Chapman

Dr. Tim Chilcott

Paul Chirico

George R. Clare

Sidney Francis Clare

W. H. Clare

R. J. Cleeveley

P. A. Clunies-Ross

Mrs M. A. Coburn

Mollie Cope

Miss H. Cope Morgan

Dorothy & Geoffrey Corney

Peter Cox

Frances M. Craig

Greg Crossan

Alice M. Crutchfield

Alan Cudmore

Peter A. Cunliffe

Mr M. P. da Costa

Jill Davis

A. Dawn

P. Dawson

Chris & Alison Debenham

George E. Dixon

Joan Downar

Mr I. Edge

Gwenyth Eggleton

Mary Elton

Mrs Dulcie D. Evans

Mr W. T. Farrer

Daphne M. Faux

Mrs E. M. Field

Ken & Charlotte Ford

Mrs G. Foster

Dr. Paul Foster
Mr R. W. Gardiner
Diana Gardner
Freda Gent
Mr & Mrs J. L. Gilbert
Mr and Mrs Robert Coles Gilbey
Hilary & Gordon Giltrap
Gill Goodridge
John Goodridge
Dr. Margaret Grainger
Mrs D. Grieves
June Grubb
Hugo Gryn
Miss F. Hackney
Mr R. W. Hackney
Peter Hague
Martin Hamlin
Miss Margaret M. Hare
P. S. Heath
Betty Hibbitt
Roy & Kate Hinchliff
Mrs S. Hobley
Margaret Holden
Mrs B. J. Holmes
G. Hughes
Mr J. Hunt
Arthur S. Hutchings
Mrs A. E. Ingham
Mr & Mrs C. A. Irons
Mr & Mrs S. R. Irons
Patricia Jackson
Miss Y. F. Jayne
Moreen Jones
Mrs D. Judd

John A. Kennedy
Dr. M. W. Kiddle
Audrey King
Dorothy K. King
Galway Kinnell
Lotte Kramer
Barry Lane
Daphne Langford
Mary Le Gallez
Richard Lessa
John Lincoln
Rodney Lines
W. G. Ling
Miss M. E. Liquorice
Barbara B. Livock
Ralph Lowings
Ann & Malcolm MacEwan
Charles Mapleston
David Martin
Miss S. Martin
Revd. A. J. McGuire
Mr M. G. Mecham
Mr R. A. Mercer
Mid Northumberland Arts Group
Graham Moyse
Mrs G. M. Mulley
Miss H. Newman
Northamptonshire County Council
Eddie Nualmanee
Oundle School, New Cripps Library
Mrs V. L. Palmer
Joyce Peach
Shirley Penny
Peterborough Central Library

Miss S. B. S. Pigrome
Roger Polley
D. Powell
Michael D. K. Price
John Primeau
Jean & Rosine Raimond
Christine Reason
Eric H. Robinson
Dorothy Muriel Rose
Freddy Rottey
Ronald J. Rule
Simon Sanada
Mrs P. Sbicca
Mick Sharpe
Peter Shaw
George Shepperson
Mrs B. Simmons
Sir Christopher Hatton School
A. J. Smith
Janice M. Smith
Mary Smith
Dr. Eleanor Snellings
Jillian Somerwill
Noel Staples
Mrs J. Stone
Mr & Mrs R. P. Stone
Edward Storey
L. D. Strange
H. Stuart Moss
Ren-ichi Suzuki
Kim Taplin
The Leeds Library
The Mount School

Denis Thomas

R. K. R. Thornton
Nancy Titman
Gerald Travers
Edward Travis
Keith Traynar
Andrew Treherne
Jean Treherne
Mrs Julia Trench
Kerith Trick
Mrs L. Wang
Gerald Ward
Helen Ward
Miss Carol Watkins
P. M. Watson
Richard Webb
Pamela Tudor-Craig
Mrs E. Wellings
Maurice West
Mike & Kate Westbrook
Mrs M. J. Wickett
Pamela Wilkinson
Sheila Willis
Mr & Mrs Brian Winder
Ellery Yale Wood
Mrs S. Woodhams
Mr R. S. Woodroofe
Mr G. L. Woolf
Mrs Joyce Wordsworth
Mary Wright
Victoria J. M. Wright
Bill Wyatt
Keizo Yamaguchi
Takashi Yamakage

PLATES

INDEX

Poem titles given in capitals; first line of extract, where different from first line of poem, in italics. Square brackets indicate that Clare did not give the poem a title.

116

SOURCES

Grainger, Margaret, Ed. *The Natural History Prose Writings Of John Clare*. Clarendon Press Oxford, 1983. *26 October 1824*, p. 193, line 19 – p.194, line 3; *4 June 1826*, p.245. lines 5–10
Personal communication: *Dog Rose*

Robinson, Eric & Powell, David. Eds. *Oxford Authors: John Clare*. Oxford University Press 1984
I Am, p.361; [*I love the little pond to mark at spring*], p.334; [*Rook's Nest*], p.274; *Snow Storm*, p.199, lines 1-14; *Song*, p.46, lines 1-8; *Song*. p.381, verses 1&2; [*Summer*], p.27, lines 1-8; *Wild Flowers*, p.353, verses 1&2; *Winter in the Fens*, p.146, lines 1-8; *Winter*, p.96; *Wood Anemonie*, p.375; [*Written in a Thunderstorm*], p.285, verses 1,2,3,6.

Robinson, Eric, Powell, David & Grainger, Margaret, Eds. *The Early Poems Of John Clare*. Clarendon Press, Oxford, 1989
The Primrose, Vol. 1 p.182, lines 1-7.

Robinson, Eric, Powell, David & Grainger, Margaret. *The Later Poems Of John Clare*. Clarendon Press, Oxford. 1983.
[*How beautiful is Sunset eye & breast*], Vol. 1. p.258.

Robinson, Eric & Summerfield, Geoffrey, Eds. *Selected Poems And Prose Of John Clare*. Oxford University Press 1967.
March 25th, 1825, p.125 lines 1-5.

Robinson, Eric & Summerfield, Geoffrey. *The Shepherds Calendar*. Oxford University Press 1964,
April, p.38, verse 6; *May*, p.51, lines 147-152; *November*, p.116, verse 1.

Thornton, Kelsey & Tibble, Anne. *John Clare: Midsummer Cushion*. MidNAG in association with Carcanet Press, 1990.
A Autumn Morning, p.458; *Emmonsales Heath*, p.160, verses 1,2,3,11,12,17; *Field Thoughts*, p.461; *Glinton Spire*, p.428; *Insects*, p.205, lines 1-8; *Memory*, p. 395; *Nothingness of Life*, p.441; *Remembrances*, p.369, verse 3 lines 1-3; *Stray Walks*, p.454; *Summer Images*, p.59, verse 27; *Sunset*, p.441; *The Bramble*, p.476, lines 1-9; *The Clump of Fern*, p.457, lines 1-8; *The Flitting*, p.216, verse 23; *The Hollow Tree*, p.451; *The Old Willow*, p.435, lines 6-14; *The Progress of Rhyme*, p.224, lines 83-88; *The Woods*, p.260, verses 1&2; *Thoughts in a Churchyard*, p.89, verses 1&2. *Wood Pictures in Winter*, p.422.

Tibble J.W., Ed., *The Poems Of John Clare*. J. M. Dent & Sons 1932.
Insects, Vol. I, p.375; *To The Ivy*, Vol. I, p.263; *Langley Bush*, Vol. II, p.101, verse 3; *Spear Thistle*, Vol. II, p.282, verses 1-3; *The Meadow Lake*, Vol. II, p.300, lines 4-11.

Tibble, J. W. & Anne. *John Clare, A Life*. Cobden-Sanderson, 1932.
The Sleep of Spring, p.i.

Xenophontos, Costas. Ed. *Life and Works of John Clare*. Xenophontos, 1966.
Fragment, p.52. verse 2.

THE JOHN CLARE SOCIETY

The John Clare Society was founded in 1981 to promote a wider and deeper knowledge of the poet John Clare, who was born in Helpston, on 13 July 1793 and died in Northampton on 20 May 1864, a most remarkable man.

The Society's membership is worldwide; support from members has enabled funds to be raised towards the conservation of Clare manuscripts in Peterborough Museum and the Memorial Plaque in the Poet's Corner of Westminster Abbey, unveiled by the Poet Laureate in 1989. An annual Clare Festival is held each year in July, and the Sociey arranges exhibitions, poetry readings and conferences. An audiotape of Clare's poetry has been made for sale. Members receive quarterly Newsletters and an annual Journal, published in July.

We welcome new members to this active society. Enquiries to:-
The John Clare Society, The Stables, 1a West Street, Helpston, Peterborough, PE6 7DU.